Grief

A Healing Words Mini Journal

Dr. Sharon T. Hinton
MSN, RN-BC, NPD-BC, D.Min, BCC, BCMHC

Memphis, TN
PepTalk Productions, LLC

For more information, email:
Staff@PepTalkProductionsLLC.com

ISBN: 978-1-959922-05-6

Published 2023 by PepTalk Productions, LLC
Memphis, Tennessee, USA
WWW.PEPTALKPRODUCTIONSLLC.COM

Cover art © 2023 Katie Silverwings. All rights reserved.
WWW.KATIESILVERWINGS.COM

Disclaimer

This workbook is designed to provide information in regard to the subject matter covered. It is sold with the understanding that the publisher and author are not engaged in providing any psychological or professional services through this medium. If such professional advice or service is required, the services of a competent professional should be sought.

The purpose of this workbook is to educate, inform, and enlighten those persons who wish to use a personal journal for self understanding, or those who may be working with such individuals professionally. The author and PepTalk Productions, LLC will have neither liability nor responsibility to any person or entity with respect to any loss or damage caused, or alleged to be caused, directly or indirectly, by the information in this book.

This workbook should not be substituted for the advice and treatment of a physician, psychologist or therapist, but rather should be used in addition to traditional medical and psychological therapies as needed.

Caution: *If you are working on major fears, family of origin, rape/incest or other exceptionally highly charged issues, it is advised that you use these journaling exercises with the guidance of a therapist or other mental health professional.*

Contents

What is Grief?

Grief is Universal

There are many causes of grief. A common reason to grieve is the loss of a loved one through death or separation. This loved one may be a person such as a spouse or close friend or a beloved pet or other animal.

Grief is also common with the loss of a home or favored location, the loss of a job, or the loss of health, or mobility. Grief also results from a loss of social connections that may cause loneliness and isolation.

Grief may be real or anticipated. Anything an individual perceives as loss or potential loss may cause grief.

Grief is Personal

People grieve in many ways. There is no one correct way to grieve and people may grieve in different ways at different times for different reasons. Culture and religious tradition also influence how a person grieves.

For some, grief is very private so outward signs of grief will not be shown in public. Some people also feel the responsibility of being "strong" for the people around them and will not show their grief openly. For others it is not only acceptable, but expected to display grief publicly and openly. This may include crying, wailing, tearing of the clothes or other demonstrations of the strong emotion of grief.

What is important is that you grieve in your own way and in your own time. Be aware that this may change over time and according to circumstance. It is okay to cry. Tears are not a weakness, but an emotional safety valve. It is also okay not to cry without feeling guilty.

Grief is Timeless

There is no time limit on grieving and sometimes when you think that you are over your grief something happens to cause you to start grieving again. This may be the anniversary of the event, a certain song, smell, or view that triggers a memory and grief begins again. This is normal and it is okay to feel grief anew even when a period of time has passed.

It is not normal to become "stuck" in your grief for an extended period of time. Feeling "stuck" is a sign that you might benefit from a professional grief counselor to help you sort out your feelings. This is not a sign of weakness or a failure – it is you acting as the intelligent person that you are and seeking help in the same way that you would seek help from a doctor for a physical wound.

Grief is Vulnerable

It is not a good time to make important decisions or great changes in the midst of your grief - there is plenty of time. Delay getting rid of a loved one's possessions or selling your house and moving until you have had time to work through your grief.

Caring people may try to be helpful by attempting to make your decisions for you. Remember this is your grief experience and decisions do not need to be made in haste.

You decide the timeline.

Asking "Why?"

It is okay to ask "Why?" realizing that there may be no answer.

Things happen.

Try hard to avoid the trap of "if only I had..." and "if only I had not...", or "I should have..." and "I should not have...".

Be as kind and understanding to yourself as you would be if your best friend was the one in your situation. Speak to yourself as gently as you would to them.

Remember, there really is *no* answer to the "Why?" question.

Grief Support

We have listed many symptoms of grief in this little journal to help you understand that what you're experiencing is normal and that it is okay to grieve in your own way. May you find comfort here.

We would also encourage you to reach out to others who will support your grief experience. Family, friends, grief counselors, and grief groups are all good choices.

Be aware that others may be well-intentioned, but uncomfortable with your grief. They may overcompensate by hovering and trying to make decisions for you or withholding information that they fear will upset you further. They may under-compensate by avoiding you because they are unsure what to do or say.

Let others know your needs. Don't be afraid to ask for company or solitude so that others know how to support you.

Signs
of
Grief

Somatic Signs

Somatic means related to your physical body. When you are grieving, you may feel symptoms like physical numbness or a feeling of unreality like being in a daze. You may experience physical distress including chest pains, abdominal pains, headaches, nausea, or GI upset.

You may also experience a weight change from overeating or under-eating, feelings of exhaustion, restlessness and sleep disturbances. These are only a few of the wide range of grief symptoms. Physical signs whether one, many, or none is a normal part of grief.

Somatic signs of grief I am experiencing are...

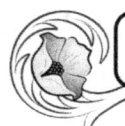

Affective Signs

Affective grief may cause symptoms related to moods, feelings, or attitude. Examples might be that you experience emotional numbness, blunting of your responses and thought processes, outbursts, irritability, euphoria or hysteria, sadness or anguish, fear and anxiety or panic, anger or rage, loneliness, or isolation. You may also feel relief, ambivalence, guilt, or even feel unaffected.

These are only a few of the wide range of grief symptoms. Affective signs whether one, many, or none, are a normal part of grief. You may also feel vulnerable at this time. Take steps to find comfort in safe, appropriate ways. Surround yourself with people who are safe and comforting.

What affective signs of grief am I experiencing?

Cognitive Signs

Cognitive relates to your thinking, reasoning, and remembering. Think of these grief symptoms as a sort of brain fog.

You may experience slowed and/or disorganized thinking, blocked thoughts (your mind may compartmentalize the cause of your grief as though it didn't exist), or even suicidal thoughts in that you wish to join the deceased or escape the situation. You may have a preoccupation with thoughts of the deceased; hearing the deceased's voice or thinking that your beloved pet or person is in the room with you.

Some people experience confusion, aimlessness, slow thinking, loss of interest in regular activities, lowered self-esteem, shorter attention span and forgetfulness. Others may be seemingly unaffected by their grief in this area. Cognitive signs whether one, many, or none, are a normal part of grief.

Cognitive signs of grief I am experiencing are...

Social Signs

Social grief includes your interactions with others. Be kind to yourself and help your friends and family to maintain positive communication while asking for and receiving the space you need.

Social signs of grief may appear as negativity in relation to others or appearing unaware of others. This may include acute sensitivity, inability to interact with others, increased talkativeness, over-dependence, withdrawal, irritability, unpredictable mood swings, attempts to replace loss by substituting another person, avoiding others, isolation, and lack of initiative or interest with social interactions or activities.

Social signs, whether one, many, or none are a normal part of grief.

What social signs of grief am I experiencing?

Spiritual Signs

Spiritual symptoms of grief vary widely based on religion, religious practices, spirituality, and perception of God/a higher power. Regardless of your concept of "God", grief may cause you to question your faith, your beliefs, and your spiritual practices. For many, spirituality provides comfort and support. For others, spirituality may cause doubts or feelings of guilt or condemnation. For some, there is a fear of becoming angry at God. It is okay to express your emotions to God in order to work through the situation. Repressed anger slows the grieving process.

Spiritual signs of grief may include questioning your faith beliefs or clinging to your faith beliefs for comfort and support. You may ask "why me?" or "what have I done to deserve this?" You may feel a sense of distance from God or an inability to pray. It is also common to have a lack of desire or an intense desire to attend religious services. Other spiritual symptoms of grief may include questioning your purpose in life, seeking meaning in your life, or growing a desire to serve/care for others. Grief may be a catalyst to grow in faith as you learn to understand yourself in relation to your spiritual beliefs. Spiritual signs, whether one, many, or none are a normal part of grief.

Spiritual signs of grief I am experiencing are...

My Grief
Journey

What is the object of my grief?

Where am I in my grief journey?

....

....

....

....

....

....

....

....

....

....

Ways that I have coped in the past include...

Is there a pleasant memory related to the object of my grief that I can write about or share with someone?

....

....

....

....

....

....

....

....

....

Who are some people I can reach out to who can help me with my grief?

❦ Dear Object of my Grief...

Note: The point of this letter is NOT to send it so that you feel free to release your feelings safely. The object of your grief can be anything or anyone.

....

....

....

....

....

....

....

....

Five Minute Focus

Set a timer for five minutes. Write whatever comes to mind. Don't think—just write. Stop in five minutes and review, circling emotion words.

What did you discover from your Five Minute Focus?

What have you learned on your grief journey?

What steps are you taking to create your new normal?

Organizations or services I can reach out to that can help me with my grief:

....

....

....

....

....

....

....

....

....

Dr. Sharon T. Hinton (She/Her) has more than thirty years of experience in faith community nursing leadership and is a curriculum writer for the specialty practice. Along with peer-reviewed articles, Dr. Hinton specializes in spiritual care topics for nurses and chaplains as well as authoring multiple journals, devotionals, and self-care booklets.

An expert in her field, Dr. Hinton is board certified in the specialty practice of Faith Community Nursing and in Nursing Professional Development by the American Nurses Credentialing Center, USA. She holds a master's Certificate in Pastoral Studies and a Doctor of Ministry in Global Health and Wholeness. She is a Board-Certified Chaplain and Supervisor for Clinical Pastoral Education.

Dr. Hinton is the Director of the Westberg Institute for Faith Community Nursing and the Spiritual Care Association Nursing Division. She speaks internationally on topics related to nursing, spiritual care and professional development.

Dr. Hinton has traveled extensively and claims both the mountains of East Tennessee and the high plains of Northwest Texas as home. She is an avid reader and enjoys exploring museums, zoos with tiger exhibits, and second-hand bookstores.

www.SharonTHinton.com

Visit our website for free writing prompts and additional journals!

Now Available!

Powerlessness: Faith Over Fear in Professional Practice is an interactive journal workbook designed to encourage the reader to explore common feelings and emotions experienced by caregivers in crisis and identify common missteps.

Discover ideas and insights on changing your perspective and then integrate steps to move from fear to faith in crisis situations.

www.ingramcontent.com/pod-product-compliance
Lightning Source LLC
Chambersburg PA
CBHW061325120626
46546CB00007B/2685